newton's law

CLANK!

by Rory Tyger

a modern bear

www.bizzybeepublishing.biz
© bizzybee publishing limited 2005
Reprinted in 2008
Printed and bound in China

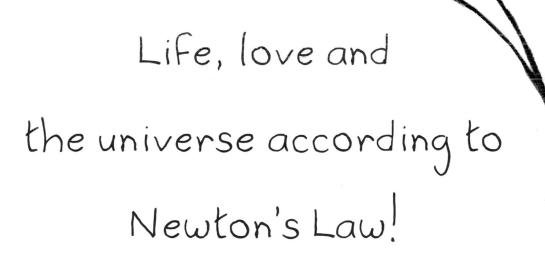

Life, love and

the universe according to

Newton's Law!

Newton's Law of life (not to be confused with Sir Isaac Newton's law of gravity, although that is pretty good too) can be summarised as follows:

"Try hard enough, don't give up and things will turn out right in the end".

This may be considered a little naive by some, who perhaps put it down to watching too many movies, but Newton's laconic wit is derived from his own life experience (and from watching too many movies!) and he has become known for his many sayings or quotes about life, which are collectively known as "Newton's Law".

life... is a puzzle

keep calm..

.at all times

Remember that life

is full of many

surprises,

but...

you've got to get in to it...

...to get something out of it.

friendship counts

little things mean alot

the future's so

bright I gotta

wear shades!

always look on the bright side because

what goes around,
comes around...

Things are looking up...

the sky's the limit, they said.

Always remember to keep

your eye on the ball...

luck is where

you find it

Remember that

life is hard

BUT....

23

24 if you can't run, you can always hide

And when sometimes
you can't help
but feel blue,
don't forget
that....

laughter is the
best medicine!

27

pamper yourself!

Don't be afraid to

show somebody

your love...

31

there's no smoke without
Fire, man!

33

let your love fly...

heart breaker

you're irresistible!

you are my sunshine...

39

I am bathing in the

warmth of your

love!

Learn how to communicate

your feelings.

It's good to talk.

hi!

now you say
something...

43

Clear your

mind.....make a list

45

If you find
yourself
getting all
tied up...

46

take time
to think..

I think I'm ge

ing in deep...

If you want to
get ahead...get
a hat

Always be number
one. Bring your
own box!

give a gift of the garden...

say it with Flowers!

Nature and Co.

Decorators of the World

57

gardens are

great to relax in

Newton's no 1 best

gardening tip...

....Don't!

give in to your creative side..

make all your good ideas bear fruit!

64

67

roses are red,

violets are blue,

some poems rhyme,

this one doesn't

If I go away

forget-me-not.....

Chocolate
does'nt agree
with me—

it brings me
out in brown
blotches...

have YOU passed the minimum stuffing requirement?

I'm doing my best....

sometimes
I need
a long lunch

77

Tea or

79

If you are going to

go out for a bite...

...don't be tempted

to eat anything

bigger than your

head

Find ANY excuse to celebrate—
champagne is 'slimming'...

86

it's not the party you're at, it's the list that you're on.

you can never have

too many presents

celebrate

in style!

music is good for

the soul...

have fun at Christmas

merry Christmas!

this is a handkerchief
waving
moment...

need a hug...

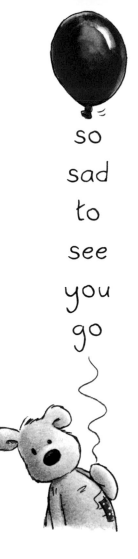

so

sad

to

see

you

go

96